CHARLES DARWIN'S
VOYAGES OF
DISCOVERY

Izzi Howell

W
FRANKLIN WATTS
LONDON • SYDNEY

Franklin Watts
First published in Great Britain in 2016 by The Watts Publishing Group
Copyright © The Watts Publishing Group, 2016

Produced for Franklin Watts by
White-Thomson Publishing Ltd
www.wtpub.co.uk

HB ISBN: 978 1 4451 4853 3
PB ISBN: 978 1 4451 4855 7

Credits
Series Editor: Izzi Howell
Series Designer: Rocket Design (East Anglia) Ltd
Consultant: Philip Parker

The publisher would like to thank the following for permission to reproduce their pictures: Alamy/FineArt 5; Alamy/ The Natural History Museum 17 (top) and 19; iStock/Grafissimo cover (right); iStock/DC_Colombia 5; iStock/mstroz 8; iStock/JohannaRalph 16 (background); iStock/gregul 17 (bottom); iStock/peterspiro 29 (left); Mary Evans/Photo Researchers 6; Science Photo Library 13 (top); Shutterstock/Route55 cover (left) and title page; Shutterstock/Triff 3; Shutterstock/marekuliasz 7; Shutterstock/aodaodaodaod 9 (top); Shutterstock/Adrian 507 11; Shutterstock/irabel8 14 (bottom); Shutterstock/Ricardo de Paula Ferreira 15 (top); Shutterstock/Ondrej Prosicky 15 (centre); Shutterstock/l i g h t p o e t 15 (bottom); Shutterstock/nito 16 (left); Shutterstock/Matyas Rehak 16 (right); Shutterstock/Ryan M. Bolton 18; Shutterstock/jehsomwang 23 (top left); Shutterstock/mexrix 23 (top left centre); Shutterstock/majeczka 23 (top right centre); Shutterstock/G. K. 23 (top right); Shutterstock/Eduardo Rivero 23 (bottom left); Shutterstock/mikeledray 23 (bottom right); Shutterstock/Giovanni G 29 (right); Shutterstock/Everett Historical 30; Stefan Chabluk 14 (top) and 20; Steve Evans 24; Wellcome Library, London 9 (bottom), 10, 12–13 (bottom), 22, 25, 26 (top and bottom), 27 and 28; Wikimedia 21 (top); Wikimedia/Biodiversity Heritage Library 21 (bottom).
All design elements from Shutterstock.

Every attempt has been made to clear copyright. Should there be any inadvertent omission please apply to the publisher for rectification.

Printed in China

Franklin Watts
An imprint of
Hachette Children's Group
Part of The Watts Publishing Group
Carmelite House
50 Victoria Embankment
London EC4Y 0DZ

An Hachette UK Company
www.hachette.co.uk
www.franklinwatts.co.uk

Words in **bold** can be found in the glossary on p30.

"I think that I am superior to the common sort of men in noticing things which easily escape attention and in observing them carefully."

Charles Darwin

Some quotes have been simplified and revised with modern spelling.

CONTENTS

WHO WAS CHARLES DARWIN?

Charles Darwin (1809–1882) was a British scientist and **naturalist**. In the 1830s, he spent five years studying the wildlife, **fossils** and rocks of South America. This trip is known as Darwin's voyages of discovery.

On his return to Britain, Darwin came up with the **theory** of **evolution** by **natural selection**, one of the most important scientific ideas of all time.

▼ During his trip, Darwin visited places such as the Galápagos Islands, off the coast of Ecuador.

HOW do we know?

Charles Darwin took notes and made drawings during his trip. He wrote several books about his **observations**.

▼ This is a portrait of Charles Darwin as a young man in 1840.

> " I think that I am superior to the common sort of men in noticing things which easily escape attention and in observing them carefully. "
>
> Charles Darwin

WHAT do you think?

What do you already know about Charles Darwin? What do you think you will find out from this book?

CHILDHOOD COLLECTIONS

Charles Darwin was born to a rich family in Shropshire, Britain in 1809. As a child, Charles loved to be out in the countryside, hunting animals and birds and collecting stones.

When Charles was eight years old, his mother died. At the age of nine, Charles was sent to **boarding school**. Charles found it very boring, as his teachers only taught him to repeat facts from memory.

► This portrait shows Charles, aged six, and one of his sisters, Catherine.

FIND OUT FOR YOURSELF
How many brothers and sisters did Charles have?

HOW do we know?

Charles Darwin wrote an **autobiography** about his life. In it, he talks about his childhood.

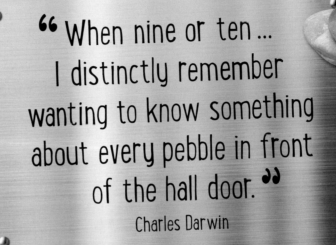

"When nine or ten... I distinctly remember wanting to know something about every pebble in front of the hall door."

Charles Darwin

▼ As a child, Charles had a large pebble collection.

AN UNUSUAL EDUCATION

Charles' father was a doctor. In 1825, he sent Charles to study medicine at Edinburgh University in Scotland. At that time, Edinburgh was full of scientists with brilliant new ideas. Charles enjoyed learning about plants and birds as part of his **degree**, but he hated studying medicine.

◀ As well as learning about the human body from drawings in books, Charles had to watch his teachers take apart dead bodies to learn about them.

RIGHT LUNG

LEFT LUNG

HEART

PERICARDIUM

DIAPHRAGM

STOMACH

TRANSVERSE COLON

SMALL INTESTINE

GALL BLADDER

BLADDER

SAPHENOUS VEIN

Charles stopped studying medicine after two years and went to study **theology** ul Cambridge University. There, he met the professor John Stevens Henslow, who helped him study plants, animals and **geology**. Charles spent much of his time at Cambridge collecting beetles in the countryside, rather than studying, but he managed to **graduate**.

◄ Charles loved collecting beetles. Once he tried to carry three rare beetles at the same time, with one in each hand and one in his mouth! The beetle in his mouth escaped.

▼ John Stevens Henslow (1796–1861) was a professor of **botany** at Cambridge University.

WHAT do you think?

Do you have any collections? What would you like to collect in the future?

A THRILLING TRIP

In 1831, Henslow told Darwin about a two-year-long trip to Tierra del Fuego, the most southern point of South America. The ship's captain, Robert FitzRoy, wanted to map the South American coastline so that it would be easier for British ships to travel there to **trade**.

▼ Robert FitzRoy (1805–1865)

Darwin was invited to join the expedition as a scientist. He wanted to collect samples of South American animals and rocks. After months of planning and waiting for good sailing weather, they set sail from Plymouth Harbour on 27 December 1831.

HOW do we know?

We can read the letter that Henslow sent to Darwin, telling him about the trip.

WHAT do you think?

Why do you think Darwin decided to go on this trip?

▼ Tierra del Fuego has cold weather because it is very far south. Water freezes into icebergs and rivers of ice called glaciers.

Cambridge
24 Aug 1831

My dear Darwin,

I shall hope to see you shortly fully expecting that you will eagerly catch at the offer which is likely to be made you of a trip to Terra del Fuego & home by South East Asia.

glacier

iceberg

HMS *BEAGLE*

Robert FitzRoy's ship was called HMS *Beagle*. It had already been used on one trip to South America. Some parts of it, such as the deck, were rebuilt to make them safer before Darwin's trip.

The HMS *Beagle* had a crew of over 70 people. It wasn't a big ship, so it was crowded. Darwin had to sleep in a hammock over a table in the chart room!

▼ This is a side view of the HMS *Beagle*. Darwin sometimes joined Captain FitzRoy in the Captain's cabin.

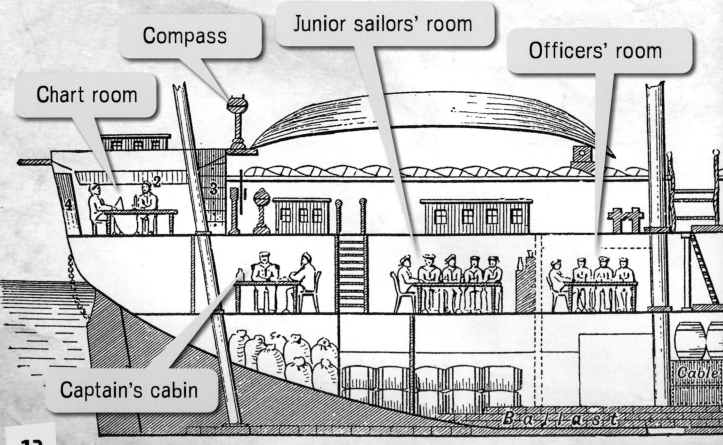

Chart room

Compass

Junior sailors' room

Officers' room

Captain's cabin

Ballast

Cable

HOW do we know?

We can see drawings and paintings of HMS *Beagle* that were done at the time.

FIND OUT FOR YOURSELF
What does HMS stand for?

Land ahoy!

◄ The HMS *Beagle* needed a large crew to operate its many sails.

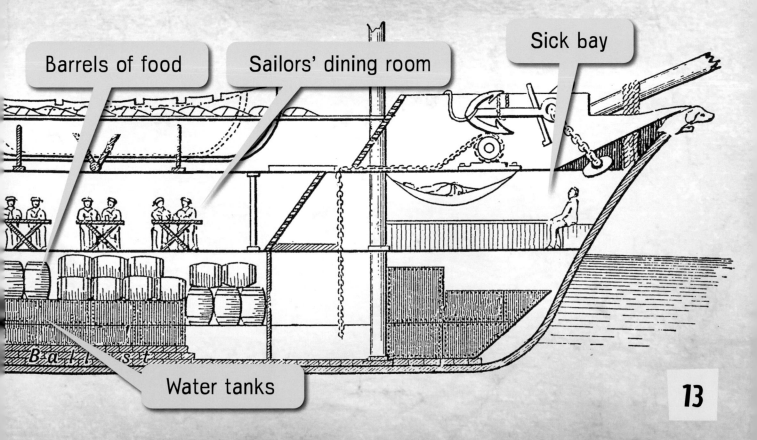

Barrels of food

Sailors' dining room

Sick bay

Ballast

Water tanks

13

SETTING SAIL

After leaving Britain, the HMS *Beagle* sailed south to the Cape Verde Islands in the middle of the Atlantic Ocean. Darwin began keeping a diary of his observations and experiences, such as his bad seasickness!

Britain

Cape Verde Islands

Africa

Galápagos Islands

South America

Outward journey of the HMS Beagle

▲ The route of the HMS *Beagle* to and around South America.

WHAT do you think?

How would it feel to be in a ship on a rough sea?

▼ Darwin felt very ill because of the rough Atlantic seas. He couldn't eat anything but dry biscuits and raisins for some time.

The HMS *Beagle* arrived in Brazil on 28 February 1832 and spent the next few months travelling down the coast. While FitzRoy took measurements for his map, Darwin explored the **rainforest** and collected **specimens**. He sent the specimens by ship back to Henslow, who had stayed behind in Britain.

◄ Darwin loved the variety of plants and animals that lived in the Brazilian rainforest.

HOW do we know?

We can read the diary that Darwin wrote about his experiences.

66 I have been wandering by myself in a Brazilian forest ...
To a person fond of natural history such a day as this brings with it pleasure more acute than he ever may again experience. 99

Charles Darwin, 29 February 1832

ADVENTURES IN ARGENTINA

By September 1832, the HMS *Beagle* had reached Argentina. There, Darwin explored the grasslands and hunted for fossils in cliffs by the sea. He found fossils of many **extinct species**, including a type of giant armadillo, later known as a Glyptodon.

◄ The cliffs where Darwin went fossil-hunting were made of soft muddy rock. He used a pickaxe to dig out the fossils.

▼ Grasslands in Argentina

Darwin noticed that the Glyptodon fossil looked similar to the live armadillos that he had seen (and eaten!) in Argentina. He sent the fossils back to Britain, but he couldn't stop thinking about them for the rest of the trip.

▶This Glyptodon skeleton is in the Natural History Museum in London. Darwin found parts of a similar Glyptodon skeleton in Argentina.

◀ Darwin ate armadillo meat with Argentinian cowboys. He thought that it tasted like duck!

WHAT do you think?

Would you eat armadillo? What is the strangest food that you've tried?

FIND OUT FOR YOURSELF
Find out the name of two extinct animals.

THE GALÁPAGOS ISLANDS

Darwin's trip was only supposed to last two years, but it ended up lasting almost five! From 1832 to 1835, the crew of the HMS *Beagle* explored the islands of Tierra del Fuego and the nearby coastline.

After that, they sailed up the west coast of South America. They reached the Galápagos Islands in the Pacific Ocean on 15 September 1835.

▼ The Galápagos Islands are home to marine iguanas. In his diary, Darwin described marine iguanas as 'disgusting, clumsy lizards.'

Disgusting and clumsy? How rude!

Darwin collected many samples of birds and other animals on the Galápagos Islands. While he was finding samples, he noticed that tortoises and mockingbirds looked slightly different on each of the islands.

HOW do we know?

Specimens from Darwin's trip can be seen in museums, such as the Natural History Museum in London.

► These lizards were collected and **preserved** in alcohol by Darwin during his voyages of discovery. Darwin also stuffed and dried samples to keep them safe.

THE WAY HOME

After leaving the Galápagos Islands on 20 October 1835, the crew of the HMS *Beagle* visited Tahiti, New Zealand, Australia, South Africa and Brazil on their way back to Britain. Darwin continued to take notes and collect samples of wildlife, plants and rocks.

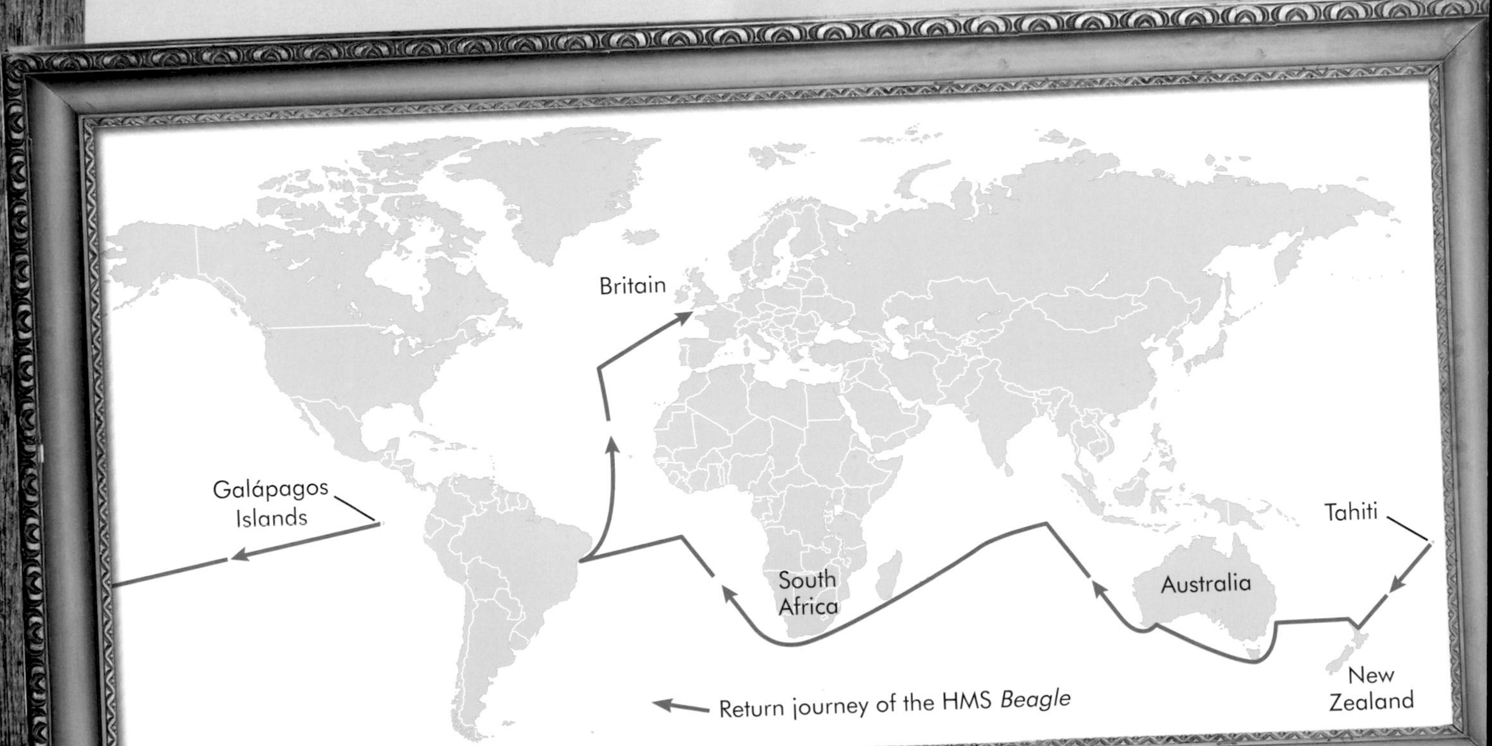

Britain

Galápagos Islands

South Africa

Tahiti

Australia

New Zealand

← Return journey of the HMS *Beagle*

▲ The route of the HMS *Beagle* from the Galápagos Islands back to Britain.

The HMS *Beagle* arrived back in Cornwall, Britain on 2 October 1836. Darwin soon became famous by giving talks about his travels and displaying his collection of plant and animal samples. He **published** the diary that he wrote on his trip and wrote other books about his experiences.

Galápagos hawk

WHAT do you think?

How do you think Charles Darwin felt when he got back home?

◀ These drawings of animals seen by Darwin were included in his books so that people didn't have to imagine what the animals looked like.

Mammalia Pl.9

Felis Pajeros

FIND OUT FOR YOURSELF
Was HMS Beagle used for more trips after Darwin's voyages of discovery?

A BIG IDEA

In the late 1830s, Darwin came up with the idea that species of plants and animals changed over time. This explained why the armadillo fossil in Argentina (see page 16) looked different to the live armadillos that he had seen.

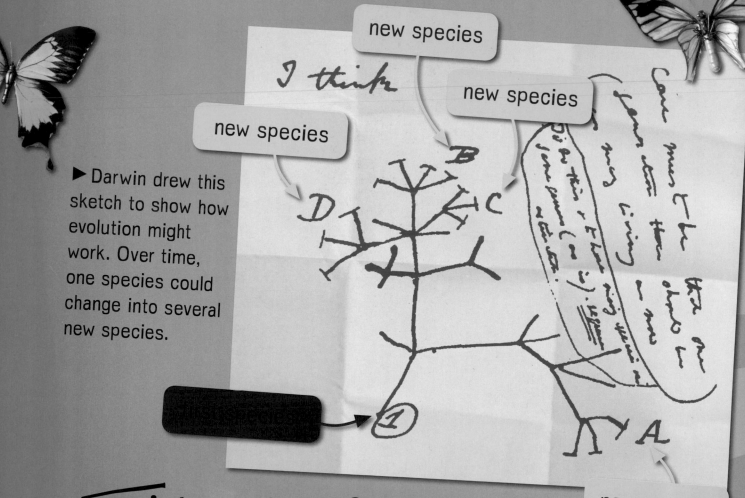

► Darwin drew this sketch to show how evolution might work. Over time, one species could change into several new species.

HOW do we know?

We can see how Darwin developed his idea from the notebooks where he wrote down his thoughts.

Darwin's idea meant that God didn't create current life on Earth. This shocked many people. Nearly everyone at that time believed the Bible story that said that God had created all animals and plants at the beginning of the world and that they had never changed. Darwin decided to keep his idea secret.

▼ According to the Bible, God created the world in seven days. He created animals on the fifth and sixth days.

On the **first** day, God created light.

On the **second** day, God created clouds and oceans.

On the **third** day, God created land and plants.

On the **fourth** day, God created the Sun, the Moon and the stars.

On the **sixth** day, God created land animals and humans.

On the **fifth** day, God created fish and birds.

On the seventh day, God rested.

FINDING PROOF

Over the next twenty years, Darwin developed his theory. He believed that animals changed over time because of a process called natural selection.

How natural selection works

◄ Sometimes, animals are born with differences that make them more suited to where they live. For example, giraffes born with long necks are more suited to their surroundings than giraffes with short necks because they can reach up into tall trees to eat more leaves.

◄ Long-necked giraffes live longer than short-necked giraffes because they can find more food. They live long enough to have young, which **inherit** their **adaptation**. Slowly, more and more giraffes are born with long necks.

◄ After thousands of years, all giraffes are born with long necks. They are all well adapted to their surroundings.

Darwin noticed evolution by natural selection in birds called finches that he collected in the Galápagos Islands. Over time, the beaks of the finches changed to suit the type of food found on the islands where they lived.

1: large ground finch – huge beak for breaking open tough seeds

2: medium ground finch – small beak for breaking open small seeds

3: small ground finch – small, strong beak for breaking open tiny hard seeds

4: warbler finch – long thin beak for catching insects

WHAT do you think?

Polar bears have thick fur that keeps them warm in their home near the North Pole. Can you think of some ways that other animals are suited to their surroundings?

SHARING IDEAS

At the same time, another scientist named Alfred Russel Wallace had the same idea of evolution by natural selection. In 1858, he sent a letter to Darwin about his ideas. Both men were shocked to find that they had formed the same theory. They decided that their theories should be read aloud at the meeting of a private science club in 1858. In 1859, Darwin finally published his own book about evolution, called *On the Origin of Species*.

Hey charles, have you been peeking at my ideas?!

▲ Alfred Russel Wallace (1823–1913)

▲ A copy of *On the Origin of Species*

HOW do we know?

As Darwin expected, *On the Origin of Species* was very **controversial** and it upset many people. However, it also became famous and sold thousands of copies.

Later, Charles Darwin developed his idea of evolution to include humans. Instead of being created by God, Darwin suggested that humans and **apes** evolved from the same **ancestor**. People found this even more shocking as it suggested that humans were no different from animals.

► Newspapers published many articles and cartoons about Darwin's theories. This cartoon shows Darwin with the body of an ape as a joke about Darwin's theory about human evolution.

WHAT
do you think?

Have you ever seen a cartoon about a news story? Do you think cartoons are a good way of learning about the news?

REMEMBERING DARWIN

Darwin continued to study the natural world until his death in 1882. During his lifetime, he caused much controversy as his theories were very different to Christian ideas about nature. However, his funeral took place at Westminster Abbey, in London, which was a great honour and sign of **respect**.

▲ Charles Darwin's funeral at Westminster Abbey

FIND OUT FOR YOURSELF
Find out the name of a place that was named after Darwin.

Today, Darwin is remembered as one of the most important naturalists and scientists of all time. His Theory of evolution changed our understanding of human history and the natural world. Some religious people still believe that God created the world in seven days, but scientists have used **DNA** to show that Darwin's ideas are correct.

► In 2000, Charles Darwin was chosen to appear on the £10 Bank of England note.

► In 1885, a statue of Charles Darwin was placed in the Natural History Museum in London. It is still there today.

WHAT do you think?

What do you think was the most important time in Charles Darwin's life? What will you remember him for?

GLOSSARY

adaptation – the process of changing to suit your surroundings

ancestor – a relative that lived a long time ago

ape – an animal like a large monkey without a tail

autobiography – a book written by someone about their own life

boarding school – a school where students study and live

botany – the study of plants

controversial – describes something that causes a lot of arguments

degree – a qualification that you get after finishing a university course

DNA – a chemical in our bodies that gives information about our genes (the code that controls how our bodies form)

evolution – the way in which living things gradually change over millions of years through natural selection

extinct – describes an animal that doesn't exist anymore

fossil – the remains or shape of an animal or plant that has been preserved in rock for a very long time

geology – the study of rocks

graduate – to successfully finish studying at university and receive a degree

inherit – to look or act the same as your parents

natural selection – the way that species of plants and animals that are suited to their habitat continue to exist, while weak, unsuitable species die

naturalist – someone who studies plants and animals

observation – watching and studying something closely

preserve – to add substances to something so that it stays in a good condition for a long time

publish – to write something that is then printed in a book, magazine, newspaper or online

rainforest – a forest in a tropical area where it rains a lot

respect – behaviour that shows you think that something is important

species – a group of animals or plants that are very similar to each other and can reproduce together

specimen – an animal or plant used as an example of its type for scientific study

theology – the study of religion and religious belief

theory – an idea that explains something

trade – the buying and selling of items or services between countries

TIMELINE

12 Feb 1809	Charles Darwin is born in Shropshire, Britain.
27 Dec 1831	HMS *Beagle* sets sail from Plymouth.
28 Feb 1832	HMS *Beagle* arives in Brazil.
Sept 1832	HMS *Beagle* arrives in Argentina.
15 Sept 1835	Darwin arrives in the Galápagos Islands.
2 Oct 1836	HMS *Beagle* returns to Britain.
1858	Darwin and Alfred Russel Wallace share their ideas about evolution.
22 Nov 1859	*On the Origin of Species* is published.
19 April 1882	Charles Darwin dies.

FIND OUT FOR YOURSELF ANSWERS

p6 – Four sisters and one brother.
p13 – Her Majesty's Ship.
p17 – Some extinct animals include all dinosaurs, mammoths and dodos.
p21 – Yes, for one final trip around Australia from 1837–1843. p28 – Some places include Darwin Island in the Galápagos Islands and Charles Darwin National Park in Australia.

INDEX